CLOWN
Joy of Failure

The Secret to Genuine Success

JOHANNES GALLI

You can view the complete program
of the Galli Publishing House
on the Internet at:

http://www.galli-group.com

or

http://www.galli.de

or

email to: publishing@galli-group.com

1. English edition 2001
All rights reserved
ISBN: 1-58619-028-8
Library of Congress Card Catalogue No.: 2001087405

Photography:
Georg Nemec

Cover and text design:
Paulette Eickman

Printed in Canada
February 2001

2505 Second Avenue Suite 515 Seattle Washington 98121 (206) 748-0345
e-mail: info@elton-wolf.com   Internet: http://www.elton-wolf.com
Seattle • Los Angeles

Author's Foreword

About the Author

Through the cellar
to the roots

Laughing on the outside,
silent on the inside

From one extreme
to another
and beyond

Mirror, mirror
in my hand

Many faces —
none that fit

The teacher's touchstone
and stumbling block

The eternal loser —
invincible

This book is dedicated
to all those who always
do the wrong thing
at the right time.

6

Author's Foreword

When I first published "Clown, Joy of Failure" in Germany in 1989, I was devoted to the idea of giving people a better understanding of the fascinating figure of the clown. At that time, I was doing a lot of acting in clown theater and also held clown workshops nearly every week. By playing the clown, the participants in these workshops had an opportunity to experience the pleasure that transforming everyday stress into delight of playing can provide. The more I expanded this range of opportunities for playing, the more levels of society the clown was able to reach. More and more interested people set out to discover the clown in themselves, or in other words, to discover the sheer pleasure of playing.

My clown work received another huge stimulus a few years ago when the fact that laughing is healthy was promoted throughout the world. Today, ten years later, my enthusiasm for the clown has been transformed into the certainty that the clown helps to develop a quality of character which is threatening to disappear — cheerful composure!

The clown I'm referring to has little in common with the entertainer in modern circuses, much however, with the jesters in advanced civilizations of the past. It was the jester's task to use his foolishness to hold a mirror before the people in which they could discover their true nature. This book illustrates my own confrontation with the clown and is intended to encourage readers to dare to do the same.

The book will help you discover and follow your own path to the internal clown lying dormant in each of us. I recommend that you open the book to the page of your choice, once a day, once a week, or perhaps only once a month, and contemplate it. Simply let the words and pictures seep in. The clown throws open a door and shows the way. It's up to you whether or not to go through. I hope, with my whole heart, that the clown will touch the hearts of all people. If that happens, we'll find ourselves in a new world.

About the Author

Johannes Galli, M.A.

Johannes Galli was born near Frankfurt, Germany in 1952. He studied literature, philosophy, and history at the Unversity of Freiburg in Breisgau. He pursued his artistic career as an actor and quickly progressed in European theater and on the cultural scene. In the 1980s, he was known throughout Europe as "Clown Galli".

Early in his training he realized, "In acting, the genuine person appears". This became the core of his philosophy in the Galli Method®, the body language awareness training which uses the light-heartedness and liveliness of spontaneous role-playing as the basis for personal growth and resolution of conflicts.

During the course of his international career as a clown, actor, director, musician and author, he has been able to test and constantly develop his communication methods in countless training courses. Several business and research trips to North America and China have allowed him to present his training technique with an international element and to create a new book entitled, *Intercultural Communication and Body Language.*

As the founder of the Galli Corporate Theater, which creates theater pieces for companies, and as the author and director of Motivational Theater, Johannes Galli has worked for prominent business enterprises worldwide. Since 1989, the demand has continued to grow for Corporate Theater presentations that are designed to strengthen intercultural bonds and mutual understanding.

Additional information about the Galli Method® can be found in the many books Johannes Galli has authored. (See page 159 for additional Galli publications.)

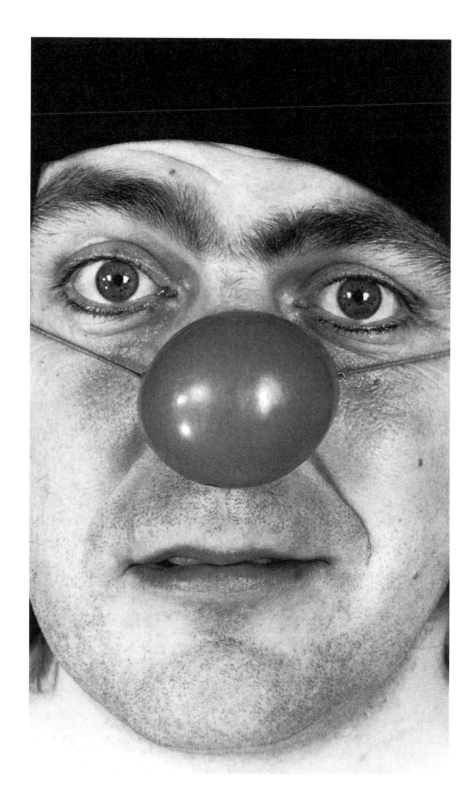

Through the cellar
to the roots

The clown is as old
as humanity.
Whether he playfully advised
the pharaohs of Egypt
or, in Greece,
relieved the tragedy
as an impromptu actor of a satire
or as a shaman "Heyoka",
supervised Indian children
and made the tribe
laugh in times of crisis
or as court jester
during the Middle Ages,
when he alone was allowed
to tell the king
the truth hidden in jokes
or as a harlequin
in the Commedia dell' Arte,
when he climbed down
from the covered wagon to mock
the authorities
amidst the shouts of the people
or today, as a clumsy oaf
in a modern circus,
tamed and robbed of his bite,
he arouses laughter from children
with his bungling.
The clown plays
into the hearts of the people.

The clown is a creator.
He continually creates
moods, characters and
brings to life
everything he touches.
He is the creator
of his whole world.
Occasionally he creates
characters
with such intensity
that he himself is startled by them.

With all his heart the clown believes
that life is given to him
so that he can amaze the world through his play.

Since the very beginning of humanity,
the clown has existed —
a part of all people.
Nothing genuine can unfold
until people see the world
anew, as a clown.

The word "clown"
comes from the Latin
"colonus", which means
"The country dweller".
What is meant is
the oaf from the country
who can never grasp
the new rules
of city society.
The clown is just as helpless
in the city
as the heart is
helpless against
the constructs of the mind.

The status of the clown within a society reflects the interest that society has in knowing the truth.

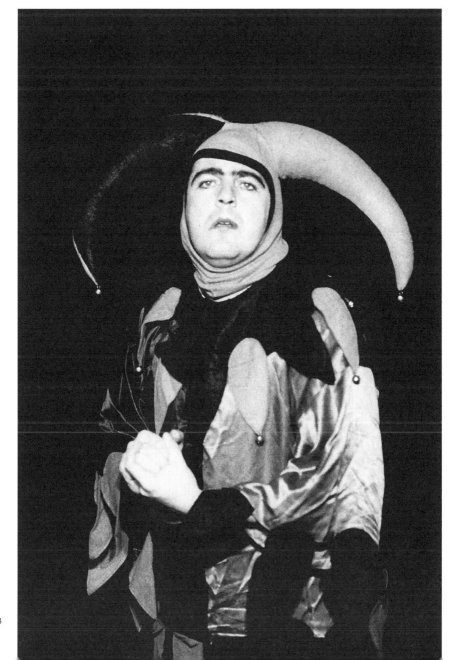

Because the clown is an actor of the truth,
he must first sense his own truth
that originates from
fairy tales and myths.
Fairy tales always portray
life's conflicts
and their solutions
which can only be acted out.
The clown,
as the main actor of
fairy tales and myths,
knows them all,
has experienced them all.
From them,
he has gained the depth
of human experience,
which he needs for all
his performances.

A clown finds his stories
in the human body,
the place
where a person
holds at bay
all the unwanted aspects of his character,
his Children of the Dark®.
The clown, however,
is not afraid
of these banished aspects.
On the contrary,
because he knows how
vital these characters are,
he lures them out and uses them to make
the most wonderful performances.

The clown plays
with the Children of the Dark®
and, in doing so,
traces their roots
right back to the mythic source.
In the same way,
he leads a person
into his deepest abyss
in order to gain
a new perspective.

In the holy rituals
of early civilizations,
the clown was the master examiner.
The neophyte priests had to
practice strict dance formations
to difficult rhythms for many years.
On the day of the examination,
the high priest
dressed himself in old, torn robes
and tried to get the neophytes
to lose the rhythm
by dancing out of step
and moving erratically.
The final examination,
before a person
reaches his center,
is the clown.

Traditional clown acts
have been performed over generations
and passed along by teachers
to their students.
All the phenomena of human existence
can be revealed in clown acts.

**Laughing on the outside,
silent on the inside**

One only becomes a clown
when there is
no other option.

Being a clown is a mood
into which one must leap.
It is just as impossible
to reach one's own clown
step-by-step
as it is
to jump over a ravine
step-by-step.
One brave leap —
and the clown is there!

The clown marvels:
I act, therefore I am.

One cannot force
the clown in oneself
any more
than one can
force love.
But just
as you hope
love will choose you
and crown you with its presence,
you can hope
the clown will choose you
and introduce you with humor
to the elevated art of failure.

To discover
one's own clown,
one must first
discover one's own boundaries.
These are
all the situations in life
that one tries to avoid.
At each moment in life,
when a person
is no longer willing to act,
he disappoints his clown.

C hildren love
the clown because
so many things go wrong for him —
just as they do for them.

The clown does everything
with genuine seriousness,
but he never takes anything seriously.

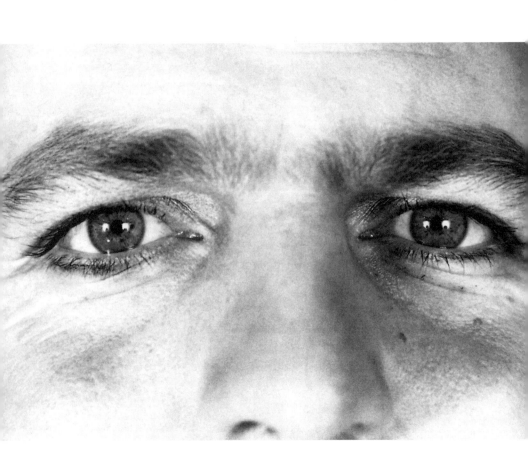

The clown doesn't
waste energy
trying to win
the favor of others.
He uses
his own weaknesses
and those of others,
without reservation,
as the guidelines for his act.
And what happens —
weakness is transformed into strength.

What makes the clown
so trustworthy
is that he cannot hide his emotions.
You can read him like a book.

Like a child,
the clown sees everything
as if it were the first time.
He looks.
His view is not
clouded
by any judgments.
That is what makes him so lovable —
his bewildered amazement.

We laugh at the clown because he takes his act dead seriously.

The clown does everything
without premeditation.
He cannot represent any
moral or political stance.
He alone is the actor
in the play.
He is not the comic herald
of a point of view,
opinion, or value.
With his red bulbous nose,
the clown is
so disfigured
that trying to take part in the
merciless race for success
is hopeless.
He has no alternative
but to aim for the top;
to put life on stage
or to even put life at stake.

The clown lives
from moment to moment,
idea to idea.
He looks for the truth not
by thinking
but by being.

Because the clown
has abandoned
the cage of the mind,
he abandons every form of
rational thought.
He submits without question
to all rules and regulations.

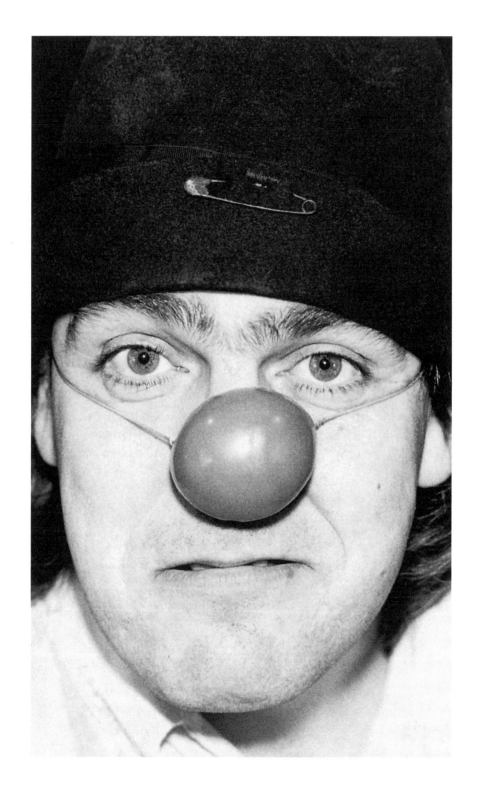

Anyone who wants to see
what a real clown looks like,
need only suggest playing
a game to a child.
What lights up in the eyes of the child?
The clown!

Everyone shakes
with laughter
at the clown,
thus creating space
in themselves
to receive his message:
The loser — invincible.

In each individual,
there lives a clown
who guards
natural impulses.
As the truth cannot be spoken,
the clown acts his way into it.

The clown reveals
his depth,
not in what he does,
but in how he does it.
He is an actor
of holistic analogy.
What he discovers innocently
in small things,
can be applied
to larger things.

The clown knows
that words are abused.
They transform
living systems
into dead structures.
Therefore he avoids speaking,
and, if he speaks at all,
he distorts the words,
giving them a deeper meaning.

A clown is the master of nothing — but a good one.

As the clown
likes to begin new plays —
he always acts his old ones
to the end.

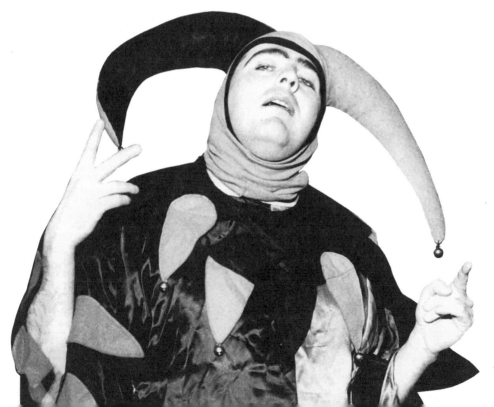

The clown has not
been granted
the gift of words.
So he talks with
his eyes, his face,
his hands,
his whole character,
and all the vocal
expressions within
the human
imagination,
in short,
with his heart.

The clown
does not play roles,
but rather,
he relinquishes them.
Only then do they
come to life.

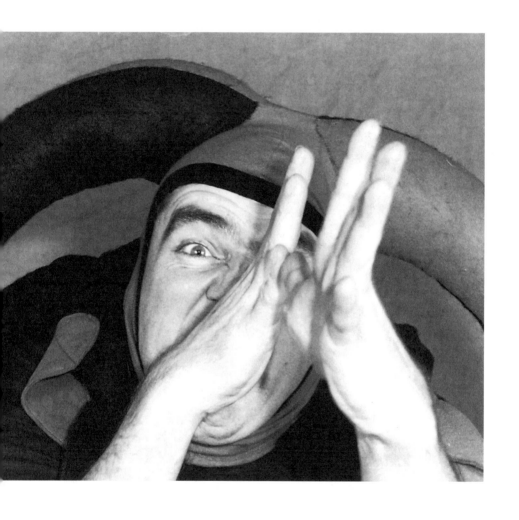

**From one extreme
to another
and beyond**

The clown knows
that people are connected
to each other through breathing.
His act breathes.

The clown loves confrontations,
so he throws himself
into every conceivable act.
The more challenging a problem is,
The more he wants to act it out.
If his counterpart plays
the weak role,
the clown plays
the strong role.
If his counterpart plays
the strong role,
the clown plays
the weak role.
He knows
that only the experience of playing polarity
paves the way for a genuine encounter.

The clown's style
consists of
the quick interplay
of tears and laughter,
joy and sorrow,
hatred and love.
When he cries,
he cries from the depths of his pain.
And when he is happy,
he is ecstatic.
The clown tries to merge
the extremes in himself
by changing moods
more and more quickly.
He becomes capable of greater and greater changes
until he is beyond change.

In his act,
the clown transforms
objects into animate beings.
He creates human relationships
with the objects he personifies.
This method is for him
a never-ending source
of new perspectives.
By mixing things up
and combining them
in the wrong way,
he makes it clear
where they belong.

Because the clown can play
all the roles,
which other people live,
he is always alone.

The clown loves
to express himself clearly,
sometimes too clearly.
He loves noise
up to the level of shrieking and raging,
just as he loves quietness
to the point of sighing without sound.
He plays with feelings
as if they were
divine juggling balls.
What he tosses away as fear —
he catches again as confidence.
He juggles
with tears and laughter,
love and hate.

In every person,
a clown waits,
hidden behind
melancholy thoughts,
to change the daily grind
into a hilarious clown number.

When in life,
"yes" and "no"
oppose each other in
deadly earnest,
the clown offers a game,
a third power,
which creates the solution.

The clown should never be mistaken for being obstinate. Contrariness provokes an encounter, but the clown is seeking an encounter because he wants to play.

To put it precisely,
the clown doesn't care,
whether he plays, or you play,
or the others play.
The clown is only happy,
when the play is on.

Mirror, mirror
in my hand

Since time began, theater has been
a sacred act
in which a person
could recognize himself.
The clown was the venerable actor
who, with his crystal clear sight
and art of interpretation,
could mirror unconscious
human nature
in the light of awareness,
and open it to laughter.
A look into his
well-polished mirror
takes away
all the illusions
about one's own existence
for a moment.
And now . . .

L augh into the mirror
the clown holds before you.

At the moment a person is being reflected,
the clown says:
"You may lack ability,
but look,
I am even more inept!"
It's only then that the awkward person
can laugh at his lack of skill.

By mirroring him,
the clown understands his opponent.
This means:
For a brief moment
he unites with him.
Then, however, he leads him further.
Being a clown means
removing oneself
from the moment,
for the moment.

The clown's number is "11",
which is formed by
mirroring "1".
This is how mirroring transforms
unity into diversity,
but in terms of its nature, it remains
simplicity.

The clown is
neither man nor woman,
but in his desire to mirror,
in a world
which is ruled by men,
the clown will take on
masculine traits.
In a society
where the feminine dominates,
the clown
transforms himself into a
female clown.

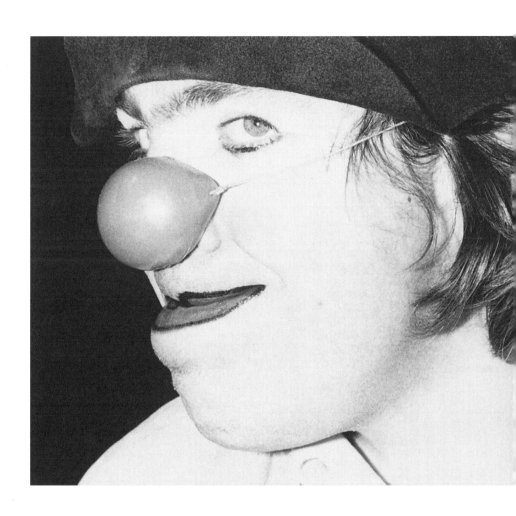

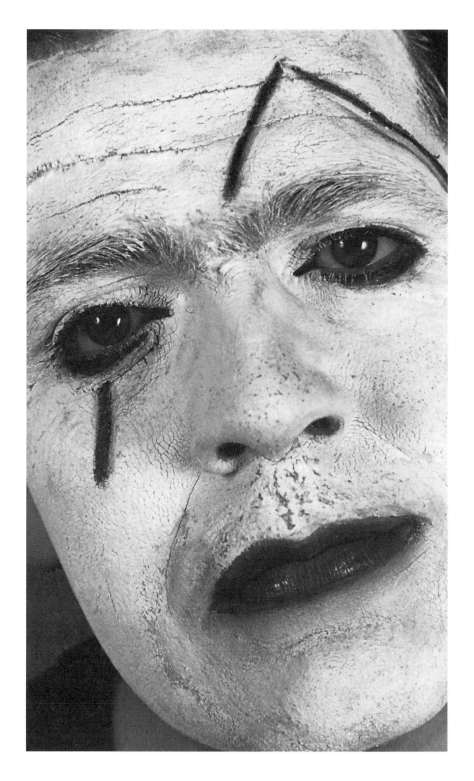

The clown loves
touching everything.
His dedication is so complete
that it touches everyone.

The Children of the Dark® are clearly reflected
in the clown's face.
He cannot and does not
want to hide them.
However, he doesn't want to
fling them out unscrupulously either.
It's in them that he seeks the tension of the play.

The clown creates
playmates for himself:
His hands, his feet,
his suitcase, his hat,
seem to be independent beings,
with whom he keeps on forming
special relationships.
His playing field is separation;
his goal, reconciliation.

**Many faces —
none that fit**

One thing connects all clowns, jesters and fools in all their diversity: Simplicity.

Stupid August
comes from the circus.
Through his clumsiness
he makes it possible,
after breathtaking
artistic numbers,
for the audience
to find their breath again
by laughing at him.

Till Owlmirror is the big prankster
of the Middle Ages.
Today, he is still known by this name
because it embodies his character.
The owl symbolizes wisdom
with roots that extend into the darkest depths
of human existence.
The mirror represents the method:
Not to talk about wisdom,
but to hold a mirror to the other person
through acting.
Till Owlmirror represents
the clown's provocative side.
Lacking a home, he moves from city to city
and tears the complacent masks
off the faces
of every person he meets,
no matter the social class.

Hans Wurst belongs to a long line of
fools who became famous.
So does Mulla Nasreddin, the greatest jester of the East,
and the Good Soldier Schweijk,
the Seven Swabians and the Wise Man of Gotham,
Punch and the Harlequin
from the Commedia dell' Arte,
whose fates have the same theme.
He is the nimble servant
who gets the best of everyone
and, in doing so, falls on his face.

Baron from Münchhausen
is considered a special
kind of clown,
who juggles so dizzily
with reality,
imagination and credibility
that the impossible
floats into the realm
of the possible
on the wings of a lie.

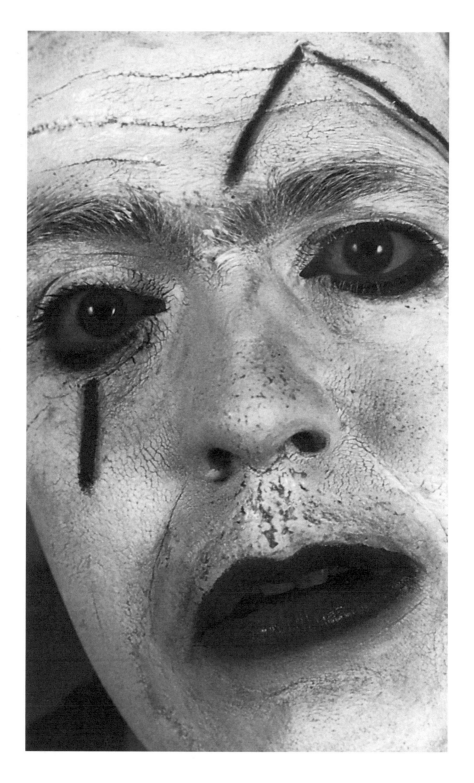

Pierrot is the sad,
wistful clown
who is filled with
unrequited love.
His drive
to dissolve himself
by melting into another
mirrors the person addicted to searching.

The court jester is the king's conscience.
In every society through history,
the clown, as the protector of truth, stood in opposition
to the ruler, as the protector of power.
The court jester of the Middle Ages
had the thankless task
of presenting the truth to the king
with a joke.
The disfigurement of the court jester
was considered a pledge that he would never aspire
to being a radiant king himself.
Playing with the truth, however,
held many dangers for the jester.
No court jester ever died in his bed.
Often he paid for his sharp jokes
with an equally sharp knife
between his ribs.

Each individual's own clown
acts in his heart.
This clown is called upon for help
far too seldom
and, often only in extreme crises.
He has such a valuable ability
to change one's point of view
on a challenging problem in life.
With a single spontaneous movement,
it appears to be a divine joke.

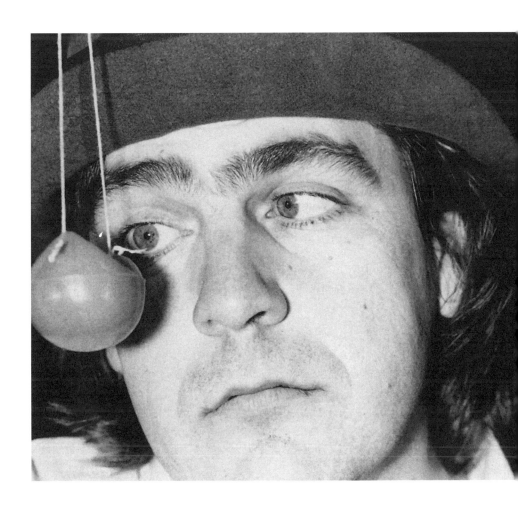

If we imagine God
as someone
who created humans
and the earth
because he wanted to
recognize himself in a
powerful play
about man's fate,
then God is a clown.

The teacher's touchstone and stumbling block

When the clown
comes up against rigid dogma,
increasing tension develops.
Acting for the sake of acting
opposes structure
for the sake of structured thinking.
Life stands in opposition to death.
The clown introduces an idea
into this field of high tension —
an idea,
that contains
the unbelievable but true solution.
Playful structure
and structured acting
are wed.

Rules are only apparent to those who fight against them.
In his act,
by complying with all the rules,
the clown renders them powerless.

By trying, unsuccessfully,
with all his power
to meet the demands
of authority,
the clown uncovers
the essential chaos
in it.

The teacher believes that he always
has to be superior in front of his class.
But, as he also
secretly feeds on the resistance from his students,
he fears the class clown most of all.
The clown takes
each of the teacher's instructions
so literally
that they are plunged into absurdity.

Because the unbearable pressure
of always having to do the right thing
destroys all liveliness,
the clown has left
the cage of pride
forever.

When dealing with authorities,
the clown behaves like a master
of the Asian martial arts,
who does not take the offensive,
but merely diverts the attack
so the blow strikes the attacker.
In the same way, authorities collapse in front of
the reflection of their miserable existence,
when a clown touches them inside.

The dogmatist entangles himself
in rules and laws.
Painstakingly, the clown
disentangles him.
For a long time, the dogmatist struggles
because he has gotten used to the bonds.
The clown wins in the end
because he has already forgotten
what it was all about.

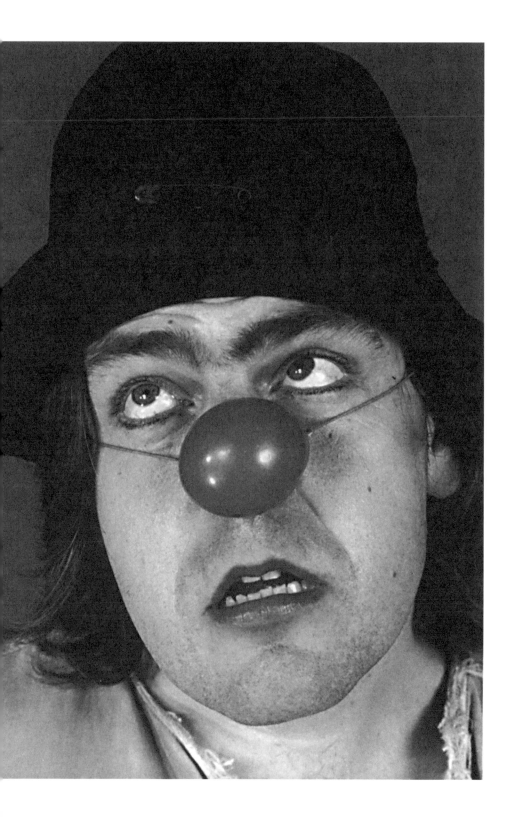

The eternal loser — invincible

The clown is
always at the bottom
of every ladder.
There, where there is
nothing more to lose
since everything has already been lost.
At the very moment
when the clown
realizes this,
he wins all
in order to gamble it all away again.

Since life ends,
briefly, with death,
the loser in a game briefly
comes closest to the truth.

For the clown, failing
doesn't mark the end of a game,
but rather the beginning of a new one.
At the moment of his bitter defeat
he discovers a new opportunity
for an even more bitter defeat.

The clown is a symbolic link
between everyday life and eternity.

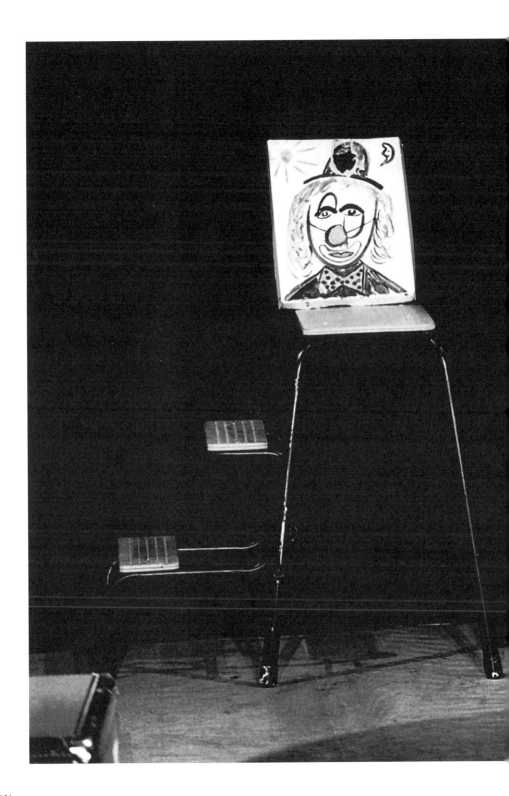

In scenes of the Middle Ages,
the jester is often shown wearing a hat
with donkey ears
and holding a child's hand.
He says,
"I alone am like
the little child!"
He is an outsider,
similar to one before him —
"Let the little children
come unto me!"

It's possible to call
the clown holy,
because nothing is holy to him.

Through his devotion to the game,
the clown, the eternal loser,
wins the strength to go on playing.
He is a symbol
of human fate,
a symbol
that neither conceals nor embellishes anything.
He simply comforts.

The *Seven Children of the Dark* in the Galli Method®

Johannes Galli believes that knowledge about human behaviour has to be presented in simple terms. During his early years in teaching and research he noted seven recurring energetic patterns emerging in people's movements and body language. He personified them and gave them exaggerated character traits so that people could act them out and be given the opportunity to transform them. This became the model of the *Seven Children of the Dark* — a central component in the Galli Method.

"Everyone has seven energy forms in their bodies. They resemble seven children — each one unique and equipped for a specific task. These children are wild and have magic powers at their disposal. Since few people acknowledge these inner children, they become wilder and remain untamed. They are also the means to access one's abundant resources of joy and creativity. In order to be happy, healthy and creative we must draw them out of the darkness, engage with them and let them grow. Most importantly, they must simply be allowed to play."

JOHANNES GALLI

Seven Children of the Dark	Transformed Energies
Slowpoke	Intuition
Bully	Initiative
Bad-Mouth	Empathy
Big Shot	Wisdom
Floozy	Passion
Miser	Organization
Loser	Bliss

The *Seven Children of the Dark* hold strong archetypal images. Galli Publishing has created a Tarot card game with a reference book for ways to use them as a creative tool for personal growth and as an oracle. Galli Publishing also has a Dance Meditation CD for the *Seven Children of the Dark* with a workbook. For further information please contact: publishing@galli-group.com

The Galli Publishing House— Teaching and Learning Materials

Additional information about the Galli Method® can be found in the many books Johannes Gallis has authored. They can be used as an interesting and informational resource for personal communication training, as well as, corporate communication training.

Additional books and other works by Johannes Galli
Intercultural Communication and Body Language
The Clown as a Healer
Body Language and Communication
Dynamic Story Telling
Communication Theater
The Seven Children of the Dark®
Dance Meditations-Movement, Butterfly, Individual Dance — Workbook and CD
Dance Meditations-Animals, Evolutionary Myth — Workbook and CD
Dance Meditations-The Seven Children of the Dark®, *Clown — Workbook and CD*
Classical German Poems with Music — CD
Traditional German Fairy Tales with Music — CD

If you are interested in more information about the Galli Method®, in the field of Galli Corporate Theater, Galli Training, and a list of products of the Galli Publishing House, visit our web site: http://www.galli-group.com

For any questions, you are welcome to contact us directly via e-mail. We will be happy to respond.
e-mail: publishing@galli-group.com

Photo Credits

All photography in this book is by Georg Nemec during clown festivals at the Galli Theater in Freiburg, Germany in 1988. The Galli Clown Festival is shown at spring carnival each year, focussing on the different aspects of the clown tradition.

In the following original clown theater pieces, actor/director Johannes Galli explored the clown with frankness and humour.

Amanda
A clown is waiting for his beloved woman. He practices hard to find the right way to approach her, but she never appears.

Photo pages: 10, 18, 26, 29, 37, 43, 44, 48, 54, 58, 69, 86, 89, 106, 109, 130, 143, 144, 155, 157, 159

Gula
A man is trapped in his own greed. His only way out is comic humour.

Photo pages: 46, 66, 103

Mrs. Gogik and Hans Wurst
Mrs. Gogik (played by Gabriele Hofmann) has the big desire to educate people all the time, until she meets Hans Wurst.

Photo pages: 33, 70, 78, 83, 90, 93, 119

Clown Mirror
A variety of unique clown characters.

Photo pages: 12, 15, 16, 23, 24, 51, 57, 60, 72, 75, 76, 84, 94, 97, 104, 113, 115, 116, 122, 124, 127, 132, 139, 140, 152

The Seven Characters
Galli plays seven human characters relating to the different planetary energies.

Photo pages: 81, 135

Clown Galli
As an audience of children watch and give ideas, he transforms into a clown and plays their story.

Photo pages: 20, 34, 38, 52, 64, 98, 148, 151

Communication Theater
Johannes Galli plays a spontaneous story created from all the ideas the audience gives to him.

Photo pages: 30, 40, 63, 121, 128